I

THE LIGHT BETWEEN US

DEDICATION

Praise Be…
for the shared
Love and Inspiration
of the
Claremont United Church of
Christ Congregational
Family of Faith.
During a time of global upheaval,
they made the choice to join their hearts,
and discovered God's Promise
of Hope and Justice
in the presence of darkness.
Their faith reflects the future
God is shaping
— even now —
where we are all
Present and Found
in the flow of
Grace.

Published by Amy Duncan
Lorton, Virginia, 22079

Cover and Book Design by Michael Kirk

Cover Photograph: "Vineyard Sunset" (detail)
by Madeleine Gallagher
Interior Cover-Page Photograph:
"Sunset Over Westsound Orcas Island" (detail in B&W))
by Madeleine Gallagher
Calligraphic Dividers by Burlesck | Dreamstime.com

ISBN-9798425854063

The publisher and the authors
have made every effort to provide accurate
transcriptions of live and unrecorded sessions.
Neither the publisher nor the author
assume any responsibility for errors or changes
that occured prior and during publication.
Further, the publisher and author
accept no responsibility
for loss or injury sustained
by any person using this book.

PRINTED IN THE UNITED STATES OF AMERICA
by
Amazon Direct Kindle Publishing (KDP)

Dear Reader:

On March 23, 2020, we came together to pray because it was the only thing we could think to do in the midst of a world broken apart by a global pandemic. As members of a progressive Christian Church with deep roots in social justice, we found ourselves struggling to understand our next steps. Seeds of despair were present and had begun to grow. The one thing we were sure of was that we believed in the power of prayer. So, on that Monday evening we gathered on Zoom to share the darkness we felt and stand vigil for those who were already suffering from the impact of Covid 19. As we saw one anothers' faces come on-screen, we took a deep breath and waded into the water — together. Yes, we showed up and God was in our midst.

We opened with a short prayer. People were invited to share their longing for others, as well as for a stronger sense of themselves. We took those natural, tentative steps as we discovered our places in this circle. And people returned the next week, and then the next, and then the next ones too. Soon, our small community found its footing and we began to wrap our virtual arms around each other. The prayers that emerged were so profound and remarkable that I found myself gathering their essences and repeating their themes back to everyone as a kind of working benediction for our time together. And contained there — in these collected and blessed offerings — emerged a practice that would come to sustain us. Each week, immediately after our gathering, I would sit with all that had been shared and listen for a "United Prayer" that accurately reflected our intentions and spoken words during our time together. Without fail, that good prayer would reveal itself within that quiet contemplation. It was not long before these outpourings of our hearts to God became an offering to the greater congregation as an integrated part of worship each week.

As the weeks turned into months... and those months came to exceed the time we ever expected we would need to be together, we experienced a veil being lifted... making multiple, and perhaps even wider, 'pandemics' visible. It was as if our prayers were unearthing more and more hidden things and then raising them up until our eyes could adjust to the bright reality of it all. What became clear was that the impact of the mounting deaths, racism, climate change and political divisions was creating ever new heartaches and anxieties. And just when we felt we had achieved a new baseline for our grief, fear and confusion... another outrage would emerge! We found ourselves leaning into, and then listening to, one another's perspectives on ways that our nation and our dreams now felt shattered. We bowed our heads to all that felt lost to us. We gave words to our grief, and during a time when words were being used to divide and injure — we found words that connected and healed. At a time when trust was eroding, we discovered God's Greater Truth.

In our love and support for one another, we found ourselves linked to a Grace we had not anticipated. Our collective sanctuary created a space in which we could gather in gratitude with others who could feed our hopes. And we found a way through; where we at first thought there was none: HOPE, despite everything, real hope, the kind with skin on it, whose caress was impossible to ignore. Our collective breathing became deeper. Our prayers took on a new intensity and we began to see God at work in the midst of chaos.

Now, collected together, these prayers reveal a unique story of Faith during this time of monumental upheaval, both social and political. Each prayer is a reminder that in the midst of all the events of life we are part of God's great Love story. It is my fervent desire that as these words are read they will take on new life, manifesting the journey of all our inner universes, guiding us to hope in the times to come.

ACKNOWLEDGMENTS

The Light Between Us grew from the experience of the weekly prayers of a sacred circle of people from Claremont United Church of Christ Congregational in Southern California. Because they committed their hearts to drawing closer to one another and to the Holy Spirit during a time of global upheaval, they learned that hope rests in a future that God is shaping with the light that is found between us.

It was the following people who spoke their hearts out loud and thus created the community that became the life source for this book: **Maria Andrade, Donna Bernard, Judith Bayer, Sandy Fasano, Linda Elderkin, Sandy Gabel, Amanda Gardner, Victor Luna, Harry McKoy, Elizabeth Miller, Rick Rogers, Jasmine Tomita, Rebecca Tortes,** and **Maria Wilson.**

We share thanks with both Rev. Jen Strickland and Rev. Jacob Buchholz, Pastors of Claremont UCCC, as well as the church's Board of Deacons, for their ongoing support.

The photographic art that graces this book so beautifully is the work of my dear friend Madeleine Gallagher. You can find more of her art at:

https://www.flickr.com/photos/mgallagher805/

You can contact her for further information with this email address:

madeleine.n.gallagher@gmail.com

Deep gratitude is given to Michael Kirk for his creative spirit and gracious shepherding of the design and publishing of this book.

When this book was a mere glimmer of an idea, Judith Wright Favor provided the spiritual companionship that nurtured that first inspirational spark.

Every creative endeavor begins in the heart, and it is the love of my family that keeps my face pointed towards the light. They give me the courage to take new adventures, showing me the way, and walking along side of me every step of the way.

THE LIGHT BETWEEN US

VIGIL PRAYERS

MAY 4TH, 2020
TO
AUGUST 16TH, 2021

HELD WEEKLY AT
CLAREMONT UNITED CHURCH OF CHRIST
CONGREGATIONAL

Lord of Our Lives:

As we live in these unprecedented times,
we seek to find our footing
as we navigate precarious ground.

We turn to you,
believing that it is your Holy Spirit
that is with us, supporting us, teaching us
and transforming us.

In prayer, we lift up:
Those who are suffering,
as a result of the impact of this pandemic.
May those who are on the front line of care
continue to be strengthened in their work
and given what they need.
All who are marginalized,
whose needs this crisis has brutally exposed.
May we grow in our feelings of compassion
and discover new ways to strengthen
our voices for righteousness.
Our feelings of guilt,
as we wrestle with our own economic privilege.
May we continue to proclaim the need
for social justice and change.
May we rise above our own discouragement.
Help us to acknowledge
our collective vulnerability

and learn that it is possible
to hold both grief and hope
together in our hands.

Lord,
we live in a space of becoming
between the life we have known
and the life that is to be.
Amen.

Spirit of Love:

We lament
the acts of violence and injustice
that have been suffered by our Black brothers and sisters.
We lament the displacement from normalcy
and the entrapment we feel.
We lament our inability
to embrace one another and express love
to our family through the intimacy of touch.
We lament our own lack of understanding
of what it truly means
to be Black in our country.
We lament the fact that we are not free
until all people are free.
We lament the polarization within our country
that blinds us to the perspectives of others.
We lament those who are incarcerated
as the result of unjust practices.
We lament the despair that weighs heavily upon this country.
We lament our own complicity
in a social order that benefits
racial and economic privilege.
We lament our own frustration at knowing
ways we can truly make a difference in this time.

Lord, we know that you hear us and,
in your presence,
we are grateful for our blessings.

May we always come to you
with prayers of adoration,
confession,
thanksgiving
and supplication.

Amen

Lord of Each Precious Life:

We lift up
all who are suffering throughout the world
during this worldwide pandemic.
Help us to remember that we belong to you.
We are your beloved children.
You have called us each by name and we shall not be afraid.
Help calm our anger
over the perspectives of others
whose point of view seems so foreign to our own.
Rather than claiming we are in the same boat Lord,
help us to focus on our neighbor's boat
and seek to understand their unique experience of this storm.
Help us to keep the faces of the marginalized
before us and offer compassion.
We lift up our workers
who give us our daily bread
and are not paid a living wage.
Help us to acknowledge our own temptation
towards "pandemic fatigue"
and give us the continued strength to behave in the ways
that protect others.
We pray in gratitude
for our connectedness to one another through this time;
for the strength we find in our gatherings,
our worship, collective prayer and communion.

Amen

Our God:

We call upon your holy name
as we deeply grieve the death of George Floyd
and the brokenness of our nation.
We call upon your holy name
to speak truth to power on behalf of all those who have died
as the result of racial violence in this nation.
We call upon your holy name in thanksgiving
for all of the young people
who have heard your call to stand for righteousness
in our communities.
Protect all who place themselves in danger
for righteousness sake.
We call upon your holy name,
to bring forward the stories of goodness,
of generosity and courage
that are being played out
in the midst of violence.
We call upon your holy name to afflict our hearts
with the pain of racism and wounds too deep for words.
As our country stands at an abyss,
we call upon your holy name
to transform our holy rage
and feeling of impotence into righteous action.
In the words of the great hymn,
we call upon your holy name

to "save us from weak resignation
and grant us wisdom for the facing of this hour."
Give us ears to hear
what people of color need us to know
and help us,
as people of economic and racial privilege,
to do the deep work of understanding
the complicit truth within ourselves.
God, hold us in our personal and collective pain.
We pray that in the midst of chaos,
your justice will reign.

Amen

Eternal Presence:

Lord, our hearts are broken,
and we pray that you will walk with us in the midst of our grief.
Lord, it feels like there is injustice everywhere
and we pray for leaders willing to do the creative work
that can truly change the corrupt social systems in our world.
Lord, your people are demanding change,
and we pray that the existing structures
of power and wealth will be dismantled.
Lord, we honor those who are champions of social justice,
and we pray for their continued health.
Lord, you have awakened us,
and we pray that as this great window of opportunity
has opened, we take wise and decisive action.
Lord, we are aware of our own despair
at not coming farther along the path of justice
and we pray that you help us have the courage
to continue the fight.
Lord, may the new learning we are experiencing
move us to places of discomfort
so that real change can happen,
and we pray to know what our work is to do.
Lord, we know that the after the marches cease,
the real work will begin,
and we pray that you will guide
the hearts and minds of your people.
Lord, many of us are wrestling with our complicity

in a system that benefits
those with racial and economic privilege,
and we pray that you will remove the barriers
to our understanding
so that we might continue to engage
in learning and deep listening
to the perspectives of all people.
Lord, our children are guiding us,
reminding us that loving one another
changes everything
and we pray that this knowledge
will transform our hearts.

Amen

God of Love and Light:

Our hearts and souls
are in the midst of transformation
and God is present to us on our journey.
Love is there.
This time in our history is helping us
to grow and change in ways we did not think possible
Love is there.
Many are having the courage to acknowledge
the systemic racism
that has been supported by the church historically.
Love is there.
Pastors are responding to the call
to support their congregations in new and innovative ways.
Love is there.
Seniors are in the midst of medical tests
and bravely anticipating the outcomes.
Love is there.
Medical teams and county health officers continue,
at great risk,
to put the lives of others first.
Love is there.
People are reaching out
to carry one another's economic
and emotional burdens
Love is there.
People are entering into
courageous conversations about race.

Love it there.
Your people are creating
spaces for human dignity
and letting their hearts
speak truth to power.
Love is there.

Amen

Our Sustainer:

We live in the promise of the peace of Christ
We pray to experience that promise of peace
in the midst of our deep concerns as the pandemic grows.
We pray to experience that promise of peace
from reading the words of wise spiritual teachers and our pastors.
We pray to experience that promise of peace
when we are physically grounded in walking and exercise.
We pray to experience that promise of peace
when we are immersed in misty morning walks
filled with delicious fragrances.
We pray to experience that promise of peace
in the midst of our gardens and through meditation there.
We pray to experience that promise of peace
when we bask in the sunlight and feel its healing beams.
We pray to experience that promise of peace
when we see the miracles of God's creation
— the butterflies, dragonflies and squirrels
that are constant in the midst of upheaval.
We pray to experience the promise of peace
found in scientific discovery and insight
with this ever-changing virus.
We pray to experience that peace
when loved ones continue to maintain their health.
We pray to experience that peace
when we are present to the unconditional love of our pets.
We pray to experience that peace
that comes in the gift of communion,

linking us
with our brothers and sisters
around the world.
We pray to experience that peace
that enables us to embrace ambiguity
in troubled times
and to live in hope.

Amen

Eternal God:

We feel like we are in the midst of chaos
and not sure of how we are going to get
to where we need to go.
Change is hard Lord and we are learning to let go.
The news of the day hits us like one wave after another
and we can hardly catch our breath.
Change is hard Lord, and we are learning to let go.
We know that new things happen only when things fall apart.
Change is hard Lord, and we are learning to let go.
Like Jonah,
we feel like we are in the belly of the whale
and we long to be carried to another shore.
Change is hard Lord, and we are learning to let go.
Our spirits are filled with noisy anxiety,
and we yearn to live in a world of possibilities.
Change is hard Lord, and we are learning to let go.
Sometimes we are worried things will not change
and we are afraid to hope.
Change is hard Lord, and we are learning to let go.
We miss our families, our celebrations, and traditions.
Change is hard Lord, and we are learning to let go.
We believe that we live in a nation whose old narrative
must give way to one whose promise
lies in the future.
Change is hard Lord, and we are learning to let go.

Amen

Holy Spirit:

Open our hearts
to the needs
of those who are most vulnerable.
Open our hearts to those who hunger
for reunions with their families.
Open our hearts to those who grieve.
Open our hearts to those who feel
alone and helpless.
Open our hearts to our emerging awareness
that this is our "new normal."
Open our hearts to hope
in the midst great discouragement.
Open our hearts to the deep resilience
of our individual and collective spirits.
Open our hearts to those
who have chosen practices
that threaten our well-being.
Open our hearts to the children
and adolescents around us
so that they can build courage for this time.
Open our hearts to all educators
as they face making challenging decisions
and creating innovative solutions.
Open our hearts to business owners
who face new closures
while experiencing limited safety nets.
Open our hearts to our country

whose ideals are at a breaking point.
And when our hearts are open Lord, may we find:
The joy of the present day before us,
our discouragement transformed,
the possibility of reinvention,
and the realization
that your sovereignty
and our love for one another
is enough to sustain us.

Amen

Lord of Our Lives:

When discouragement grips our souls,
Walk with us.
When we are overwhelmed
by the impact of Covid-19 on the lives of others,
Walk with us.
When we watch those we love take their last breath in this life,
Walk with us.
When the decisions of our leaders leave us heartsick,
Walk with us.
When we hurt for children who are not experiencing
the warm and nurturing power of the classroom,
Walk with us.
When we experience sadness for the most vulnerable of our children
who are missing experiences of loving adults in their lives,
Walk with us.
When, in the midst of anti-racist work,
we are confronted by our complicity in oppressive systems,
Walk with us.
When we see college students' life-affirming experiences cut short,
Walk with us.
When our hearts are filled with worry
for the health and safety of our children and grandchildren,
Walk with us.
When we hear the cries of those who cannot find employment
and live in anxiety,
Walk with us.

When we acknowledge our need
to protect the sacredness of the earth,
Walk with us.

For it is in our walk with you
that our hearts
can transcend our separateness
and connect with the spirits
of those in pain.

Amen

Living God:

When we find ourselves distressed
by the brokenness of the world,
we trust in your grace.
In the midst of our deep grief and anxiety,
we trust in your grace.
As we honor those who live the promise of the Beatitudes
in a world that celebrates wealth and power,
we trust in your grace.
When we are distraught
by our disconnection with our loved ones,
we trust in your grace.
For hospital staffs that must be the hands and voices of comfort
to those who are facing their last days alone,
we trust in your grace.
As we seek new ways to develop
systems of support and connection with others,
we trust in your grace.
When we confront the agony of loved ones
struggling with addictions during this time,
we trust in your grace.
For those receiving medical test results
that are cause for rejoicing
and for those whose results confirm their worst fears,
we trust in your grace.
As we watch our teens
who are just getting their wings,
experience isolation and hopelessness,

we trust your grace.
As we acknowledge those
who are facing grave financial setbacks
and to the wellbeing of their families,
we trust in your grace.
As we seek to heal this planet
that we have so abused,
we trust in your grace.

Your grace reminds us
that we are meant to be
the salt of the earth
to one another
and in doing so,
we can lift one another
to the light.

Amen

God of Light:

Our journey with You
is the story that grounds our lives in hope.
You are the light that guides us through the deep darkness of despair.
You are the mender of lives that are impacted
by the health crisis of Covid-19.
You are the net that is cast across great distances
to bring families together.
You are the great comforter to those who live
in the depths of isolation.
You are the wellspring to all who face economic instability.
You are the calm for parents of children with disabilities
whose emotions are stretched thin.
You are the champion of those whose education
is impacted by the great inequity of the digital divide.
You are the voracity of scientists whose safety and credibility
is in jeopardy as they work to reverse the pandemic.
You are the protector of public servants and postal workers
whose efforts preserve the democratic process.
You are the strength manifested in all people of good will
who are speaking truth to power.
You are the vision for those marginalized,
whose lives can so easily fall through the cracks.
In You, we experience the gift
of your compassionate witness to the needs of all.
May our hearts, warmed by your love, build a bridge
through this time to a better and kinder world.

Amen

Creator God:

In chaos, you birthed the world into being
and it is your spirit that shines in us,
we bear your light.
Dreaming that one day our country can be a place
of equity and hope in the world,
we bear your light.
Making wise decisions
about the safety and security of children
as the school year begins,
we bear your light.
Supporting children who feel the loss
of face-to-face human interaction
with friends, teachers, and extended family,
we bear your light.
Encouraging teachers and administrators struggling
to do their best as the face of education changes,
we bear your light.
Praising our Pastors and church leaders as they support
our family of faith through this tumultuous time,
we bear your light.
Gathering in prayer on behalf of those
who are experiencing suffering,
bringing peace and hope to their spirits,
we bear your light.
Holding our judgements of others
and seeking to use words of kindness and respect that honor all,
we bear your light.

Seeking comfort for those who feel the loss
of physical touch, comfort and care,
we bear your light.
Creating brave spaces for people to grow
deeper in their spiritual life,
we bear your light.
Mourning for those who feel isolated,
fearful and are dying alone,
we bear your light.

When we are light to one another,
we enter into places of pain and sorrow
with compassion and strength
that bring healing to our troubled world.

Amen

Precious Lord:

Into your hands
we commend the network of ordinary people
whose courage sustains us
through the historic times in which we live.
Into your hands we commend our exhaustion, our heaviness,
our discouragement and divisiveness.
Into your hands we commend people of courage and compassion
willing to engage in the work racial reconciliation.
Into your hands we commend our leaders,
as they return to Washington with the responsibility
to ease the economic hardship of marginalized people.
Into your hands we commend the safeguarding of voting rights
and access for all.
Into your hands we commend teachers across the country
who are bravely teaching in new and innovative ways.
Into your hands we commend teachers and administrators
who are compelled to open schools
that they fear cannot be fully safe.
Into your hands we commend educational support staff
who are the emotional lifeline for students.
Into your hands we commend parents who feel the weight
of heavy responsibility as they juggle work, school,
and the well-being of their family.
Into your hands we commend those who prize
their personal freedoms over the health and safety of others.
Into your hands we commend people who suffer the impact
of global high temperatures, raging storms and torrential fires.

Into your hands
we commend political leaders
whose eyes must be opened to see beyond
their own agendas to the
pleas of those who depend upon them.

When our own hands are empty Lord,
it is yours we seek.
In your hands,
our spirits experience an expansive space of hope.
There, we refresh our souls
and know that there is something new
waiting to be born beyond
our present sorrows and concerns.

Amen

Source of Life:

We are a people
filled with anguish and agony
over our hurting world.
Help us live out our faith
with the knowledge
that you are our refuge and strength.
We are a people dismayed
by continued racial violence and disregard for human life.
Help us invest in the deep and visionary work of social justice.
We are a people whose childrens' world is turned upside down.
Help us instill in them the power of resilience and hope.
We are a people burdened by the caretaking others.
Help renew and enrich our spirits.
We are a people whose personal stories
of disappointment, loss and grief are a heavy weight to bear.
Help us, as people of compassion,
to grant one another grace.
We are a people whose collective consciousness
supports unjust policies and practices.
Help us ignite change through your transformative love.
We are a people who are guided by divisiveness
and hostility towards those whose views differ from ours.
Help us to tear down the fences
we have built in our hearts.
We are a people who are losing their neighborhoods
and precious resources to destructive fires.
Help us heal the scars in their wake

and bring blessings to those
working courageously to protect us.

We are a people who have neglected
those who live on the margins of our communities
and those with mental and physical illnesses.
Help us bring liberation and light
to all in need without reservation.

Holy Spirit,
we know that You are at work in the world
making all things new.
In you, we are no longer afraid.
In you, we find peace and wholeness.
In you, we can see a world reborn
where all life is sacred,
all have dignity,
and all are safe.

Amen

Transforming God:

You suffer with us.
You see us swimming in a corrosive sea of lies
and discouragement.
You see the tears
that are caught in our throats
for lost lives we cannot mourn.

You see our spirits filled with contagious animosity.
You see our wounds,
sometimes too deep for words.

You see the days
where it is all we can do to keep going.

Help us to breathe you in Lord
and in that space find your holy resilience
that does not know weariness or fear.

So we can see you at work in the world
through countless acts of kindness.
So we can see your hope alive
in the darkness.

Lighten us up Lord,
so that we can be light to others.

Amen

Giver of All Good Gifts:

In the midst of our uncertainty and our grief,
we beg you, how long must we wait?
How long, O Lord,
before we become a reconciling people
to those we have hurt by the social systems we have perpetuated?
How long, O Lord,
before students and teachers can gather safely
and learn with one another?
How long, O Lord,
will our cities experience the deep suffering
reflected in protest marches?
How long, O Lord,
will the families of those who have little means
to provide funeral costs or lack of documentation
to accompany their loved ones to their final resting place
needlessly suffer?
How long, O Lord,
will we as a world community
live in fear of the impact of the effects of the pandemic?

We wait on you, O Lord,
because our faith tells us that: In you,
we can confront suffering and persecution
for all those who live in the margins.
In you, the true facts of our history as a nation
are revealed so that the achievements of all
can be acknowledged and celebrated.

In you, we see the wisdom of science
and learned people as the source of our decision making.
In you, we can take action
so that all people have economic security
and equal treatment under the law.

In you, we believe that all people carry your goodness.
In you, we know we must hold onto one another's hands in love.

We wait on you, Lord
because you live in our every breath,
as our ever-present God who abides with us always.
We wait on you, Lord
because we know your love is constant,
and that your truth
is being revealed in each moment.

Amen

God of Mercy:

When our minds are racing,
our hearts are pounding
and we feel out of control,
heal us in the broken places.
When fires ravage our land,
our hearts and our spirits,
heal us in the broken places.
When we struggle
to maintain our priorities
and fatigue feels bone deep,
heal us in the broken places.
When darkness and worries
take hold and we beg
to know "How long O Lord?"
heal us in the broken places.
When our emotional reserves are depleted
and we are on our last nerve,
heal us in the broken places.
When we break our solidarity
with the human family,
heal us in the broken places.
When we have absorbed all of the pain
from those around us,
heal us in the broken places.
When the lack of value for human life and dignity
takes our breath away,
heal us in the broken places.

Help us to breathe deeply.

Help us to rest.

Help us to ground ourselves
in your blessed grace.

Help us to embrace our flaws and imperfections,
knowing that in your love,
we will become stronger in the broken places.

Amen

Holy Wisdom:

May we be present
to all that is before us, God...
in fires that scorch our land,
in grief that holds us in its grip,
in the loss of great champions of justice,
in collective fear, anger, and sorrow.
We live in a time that feels devastating,
but it is the all the time that we have.
This is our "Holy Actuality."
A time already blessed by God.
A time of letting go
of that which no longer serves us.
A time when our longing for community
increases our capacity to endure.
A time of planting seeds for future generations.
A time filled with the spaciousness of Divine Truth.
Our precious children are watching closely
to learn the lessons of what happens when things fall apart...
that people of faith hold the center together,
that people of faith pick up the torch
passed on to them by their heroes,
that people of faith live in hope and promise,
that people of faith risk
opening their arms to be embraced by love,
that people of faith see a "Holy Now"
where something beautiful is waiting to be born.

Lord of our lives,
give us the strength and wisdom
to live into this promise

Amen

Faithful Lord:

Are you running with us Jesus?
We are running from pandemics,
from fires, from racism, and from injustice.
We have lived life as sprinters
and thought the finish line was within our grasp.
Now, we find ourselves in a long-distance race.
We are not sure that we can be marathoners.
We are afraid that we are running on empty.
Run with us Jesus!
There are those who raise their head above the pack
to take the lead.
Take their hand, Lord.
Give them strength and wisdom.
Help them to know
that none of us really cross the finish line
until everyone crosses the finish line.
Run with us Jesus!
Remind us,
that we have been created for just this time.
We have all that we need.
Through you we are embodied
with the renewable strength that endures.
May we, in faith, go the distance in the race set before us.
Run with us Jesus!

Amen

Source of Strength:

There are times we cannot find you, Lord.
It feels like a game of "hide and seek."
"Ready or not here we come!"
And you always find us,
just as we are.
When we are faced
with worrisome moral decisions,
When our neighborhoods are smoke infused
and violence torn,
When going to school and working from home
is more than we can bear,
When we are in harm's way,
When we are journeying into a fearful unknown,
When we are waiting to recover,
to heal, and get back to normal, and,
When we are discerning the awesome responsibility of our vote.
Give us new eyes to see you in the hidden places.
Remind us that your burden is light and longs to be shared.
Discern within us what is ours to do
and what belongs to you.
Help us see you in the holy spaces
you place in our midst
You made us to be enough.
We are seeking you, Lord!
Ready or not here we come!

Amen

God of Grace:

We can see it shimmering there,
just below the surface.
Your promise lies there beneath the fray.
It is Your wisdom whispering to us of life itself.
We can hear it if we breathe deeply
and listen for you in the silence.
Beyond the clamor of discord,
hatred and violence,
new ways of life are coming into being.
It is there in the birth of babies,
of love being celebrated,
of birthdays honored and achievements acknowledged.
Our bodies are responding
to the change of season and welcomed coolness.
Our spirits are filled with gratitude
for those who work tirelessly
to meet the needs of others in this time and place.
We rejoice in the comfort of fellowship
and are grateful for open and affirming hearts.
We must turn now to humility,
the voice that always speaks loudest to power.
We can only see it when we choose to pay attention
to what matters to you.
It is your world there,
Lord—full of human dignity,
compassion, love, and peace.

Amen

God of Hope:

Perhaps you gave us two hands
to remind us that your love always offers
another way to see the world?
When we feel fear, you offer perfect peace.
When we see hate, your tenderness is at work in the world.
When we feel trapped, you make all things new.
When we see divisiveness, you offer a radical welcome.
When we feel parched, you offer living water
When we see places of despair, you promise hope.
When we feel fragility, you offer compassion and strength.
When we feel overwhelmed by paradox and unknowing,
you hold us firmly in your embrace.

These times teach us that the same light
that illuminates the darkness, also casts shadows.
We are on a wilderness journey that demands
we use both hands to acknowledge the current reality
of our lives as well as celebrate a new way of being.
We are learning that our hands can hold tightly
to what is important
and they can also release what no longer serves us.
Our two hands are helping us to find our way safely in the dark.
Help us to hold ambiguity gently.
Make our spirits transcendent,
so we can travel through these times
at the speed of our souls.

Amen

Everlasting God:

Could you give us the kind of vision
that allows us to see what lies further down the road?
We see clearly what is just before us:
more injustice, more scorched earth,
more powerful storms and increasing political strife.
We see clearly what is behind us:
heartache, loss, loneliness and fatigue.
If we could see what is around the next corner,
perhaps we might not be afraid.
Being caught between one critical event
and the next fills us with anxiety.
Yet, being afraid keeps our lives small
and your love invites us to live large.
Perhaps, what is around the next corner
is the path we have been waiting for.
Perhaps we are being transformed
in ways we can't even see.
The present moment is vision enough.
It is a space not tainted by worry or regret.
Help us, Lord to fully live out of that space.
Our life is a journey towards wholeness,
and you promise no derailment.
We don't have to see the road ahead
because you are already there waiting for us.
We don't have to seek you,
for you are already here.
So, we answer your invitation to:

Dance now!
Love now!
Play now!
Create now!
Live now!

Amen

Eternal God:

We are supposed to be a people of hope.
But hope seems to be playing hide and seek.
We don't know what tomorrow holds.
It looks like it will take us longer
to heal from the grip of violence,
terrorism and fear that surrounds us.
Perhaps we can hear your message of hope again
if we drown out the all of the clamor and lies.
If we still our racing hearts and fearful spirits,
we can surely hear your voice!
We will hear that living in hope is your promise for these times.
Because people of hope see beyond their present circumstances.
We will begin again
and harness our imagination
to become co-creators of hope with you.
We will channel the spirits of saints,
who in times of previous anguish,
reclaimed and proclaimed your truth.
We will feed our souls on hope.
We will see hope in the faces of those we love.
We will see hope in the beauty of your creation.
We will capture hope in the wholeness in our hearts.
And then,
we will dispel the darkness
and point others toward the light.

Hope means
that no matter what happens tomorrow,
we are held in love.
Hope will carry us
beyond these times
to a world filled with your grace.

Amen

God of Light and Love:

We live in Holy times.
We are learning that Holy times are never neat and tidy.
They are dynamic, challenging, chaotic and surprising.
Even elections that bring a spark of hope for the future
cannot bring about all magical changes we seek.
The work of reconciliation and love continues.
But today, with joy, we can proclaim what we know:
that in such Holy times,
we are always immersed in your light.
And those who embrace this light
are asked to shine it extravagantly
on the lives of others.
Our light frees spirits filled with despair.
Our light brings hope to the unhoused,
the lonely, and those who are ill.
Our light gives energy to those who are filled with fatigue.
Our light bridges the political chasm that separates us.
Our light brings compassion to those in the margins.
Our light soothes wounds and calms fears.
Our light softens hardened hearts.
Our light allows us to bend close to listen
and open our hands in love.
It is our gift to be light bearers
and we praise you for giving us lives
that are illuminated from within.

Amen

God of Truth:

In these worsening pandemics
we often find our hearts and minds in two places.
Like our country,
we find ourselves straddling a deep divide.
At one moment we are losing our footing
and then, miraculously, we find it again.
At one moment
we can't stand the chaos and the lying any longer
and then we find strength
as we lean into our discomfort.
At one moment we are petrified
about what the future will bring
and then then we find something joyous
to cling to in the present moment.
At one moment we are horrified
by the deadly cost
of not living in community with one another
and then someone's kindness reminds us
that it is our very connections that save us.
At one moment we feel deep sadness
as we abandon our holiday traditions
and then find possibilities
in celebrating in simpler, deeper ways.
Indeed, we are living in the palpable gap
between our ideals and the reality of before us.
Doesn't your love fill that gap?
Isn't it your light that heals all divisions?

When we stand with you,
we are once again on solid ground.
When we stand with you,
we are on holy ground.
When we stand with You,
we are indeed
at the threshold
of your kin-dom.

Amen

God of Abundance:

We are having to dig down deep
to get a grip on Thanksgiving this year.
What can we do
when we can't celebrate as we want to?
What can we do when others celebrate
by disregarding the well-being of others?
We want Thanksgiving to be
the same as it has always been
and we are filled with sadness.
Perhaps,
we have taken the meaning
of this holiday for granted.
Perhaps,
we live in a "gratitude gap."
In a land filled with abundance,
people are going hungry.
In a land of opportunity,
people are struggling
to earn a living for their family.
In a land of freedom,
children live in cages
and immigrants are oppressed.
In a land of promise,
people are despondent and hurting.
You are greater than this
and call us to lean into these times
with a brighter vision.

You remind us
that being thankful
in challenging times
is the birthright of your people.
So,
we will keep the thanks coming.
We will keep the giving coming.
Together,
we will fill the gratitude gap.
Because it is in the act of communion
that we truly share
the Thanksgiving feast.

Amen

God of Hope:

Here we are!
We are just waiting!
More than any other time we can remember,
we are eagerly counting down
the days of Advent.
We are so ready to move on
from this current way of being.
How can such a hurting world
give us what we need?
So, now you invite us
into another season of waiting
—a time of anticipation
that something new is being born:
...Born for the world
...Born in us
...Born in our friends and family

There is richness in this season
of anticipation and so,
we wait in hope.
In waiting,
we call upon a much-needed stillness
and deepen our devotion:
...Beyond politics
...Beyond lies
...Beyond power
...Beyond self-interest

This is the good news
for all called by you
to be patient.
In waiting,
we live in hope.
No matter the circumstance,
God takes our offerings
of love and multiplies
each and every gift:
...Each kindness
...Each act of compassion
...Each offer of forgiveness
...Each heartfelt connection
Perhaps in this Advent season,
our waiting
will introduce us
to a resilience
that our souls
did not know existed.

Good things come to those who wait!

Amen

God of Joy:

We carry the weight of dark times
and yet here we are
in the midst of the Christmas season.
This year the gifts we seek
are real solutions and real change.
We are so focused upon
what needs to be fixed
that we forget that God
came to us as a helpless baby.
If we let go of our expectations,
perhaps we will find ourselves
in awe of the simplicity
that is the Christmas story.
There is nothing passive
about the waiting
that occurs during Advent
when we seek love born anew.
God said yes to becoming human.
Alleluia!
This is the great gift!
The Christ Child comes again to earth
in the midst of darkness bringing hope
Especially now.
Especially here.
Come Emmanuel, Come!

Amen

Living God:

We are caught between
the depth of despair
and the horizon of hope.
We are reeling
from one traumatic event to another.
We take our privilege for granted.
We have not been able to grieve
for the lives that have been lost in our nation.
As we gaze into the darkness,
is it the womb or the tomb we see?
Advent directs our hearts
to find what is being born anew.
So, we empty ourselves
of all anxiety
to make space
for God's radical unity with us.
Let us live with new hearts
Filled with:
Gratitude,
Simplicity,
Justice,
Faithfulness,
Perseverance,
Righteousness,
and
Peace

These
are the Christmas miracles
born in us.
Born in their own time,
Born with their own gifts,
Bathed in love.
The invisible
becoming visible.
Giving personhood
to the light!

Amen

Spirit of Love:

It is the longest night of the year.
It feels like we have been groping around
in the dark for so long now!
We want to break free,
but we can't seem to find the light.
In darkness,
our broken places feel more acute.
Our fears take on a new intensity.
Our souls are in great need of illumination.
We are falling on our faces
because we have not fallen on our knees.
Yet, here, on the darkest night of the year,
there shines a bright light in the heavens.
The same star that announced
the coming of the Light of the World.
We follow the star to Bethlehem
and behold that darkness never wins.
And we join the angels to sing your glory.
So, we step out in faith;
one foot in front of the other.
We are not alone.
We journey to Bethlehem
hand in hand.
Guided by the light.
Guided by hope.

Amen

God of New Life:

We are walking our weary souls
to the finish line of the year 2020.
We have been on a journey that we did not seek.
Like other travelers on paths unknown,
we have jettisoned the things
that did not serve us well.
Like explorers in a new world,
we have made unexpected discoveries.
This year...
In the midst of despair,
we have trusted prayer
to bring us into active engagement
with your grace.
In the midst of selfishness,
we have recognized ourselves
as members of one global family.
In the midst of confusion,
we have renewed clarity
about the focus of our lives.
In the midst of destruction,
we have seen evidence of life-giving acts.
In the midst of racism,
we have expanded the inclusiveness of our hearts.
In the midst of darkness,
we have cultivated our spirits
and found joy in things we took for granted.
In the midst of violence,

we have found ourselves
to be living sacraments,
healing a hostile world.
In the midst of isolation,
we have found
new ways to connect,
spirit to spirit and soul to soul.
In the midst
of confusing contradictions,
we have found a truth
that sets our hearts free.
You have made a path for us
where one did not exist.
You have held us
when we have thought another step
was not possible.
And in our weariness,
hope awaits,
and your hope never fails.

Amen

Lord of the Universe:

We are staring into the great chasm
that divides our country.
Whether we walked,
crawled or were dragged here
we are horrified at its depth
and ugliness.
Together we behold the consequences
of our collective actions.
Social norms tell us
to choose a side and defend it.
Whose side are we on?
Who do we belong to?
As a people of faith, our allegiance is clear.
The world does not define us
—who we are lives and breathes in your spirit.
And in that definition,
we become part of a story greater
than any of our current events.
The signs are clear,
it is time to quiet the noise in our heads,
rise, and listen to the wisdom of our hearts.
It is time to shout our prayers to the open sky
that we will begin to live out the promise of our nation by:
seeking justice,
practicing compassion,
walking toward one another in love,
and living in hope.

We dare to stand
in the abyss
and know
that we are in a place
where you
will most certainly meet us.

Amen

Transcendent God:

Isn't every moment precious?
So why do we rush past it
to find the next best thing?
Fearing the future
robs us of our present joy.
If we scan our souls,
is happiness available there?
We even miss the very things we complained about last year.
We are weary from chasing
the things in our life that we don't have.
This most remarkable time in history
is a wake-up call to live every moment with intention.
We have been given the space to find our true identities.
Nothing could have prepared us for this time,
and we become open to the workings of your Holy Spirit.
When we change our story,
we change the world.
Taste the present time.
Taste the present moment.
In this space we dig deep
finding you're your presence.
When we settle down,
we can reclaim the gift of now.
Change our mind
and change our hearts.

Forgive us
when we let the external circumstance
determine our state of mind
rather than our internal life
that is filled with your transcendent joy.

Amen

Lord of Infinite Grace:

Our inaugural poet
has used her prophetic voice
to challenge our nation to "be the light."
O Source of infinite light,
we are inspired
but we confess that we need your help.
We allow choices,
conscious and unconscious,
to rush over us.
We allow acts of injustice
to drag us down.
We allow external events
to manipulate our happiness
and contribute to our pain.
We wrestle with control,
fear and insecurity.
We dim the light
we have been given.
And we feel weary,
broken and lost.
Rekindle our light.
Our children are watching.
When we feel fragile,
place us on solid ground.
When we have finite strength,
give us infinite love.

When we feel the anguish
of confusing promises,
show us the way.
Our children need to see us choose light.
They need to see that hope
is alive in this new day
filled with imagination.
Perhaps your Kin-dom is closer now.
As close to us as breathing.
We are aglow
in a way that is internal
and eternal.

We are light with skin attached.
We are your light to the world.

Amen

Holy God:

We think we can see the light
at the end of the tunnel.
We want to relax and let our guard down
and yet, we are called to be vigilant.
It has been almost a year since we were called inside.
Even though we see our freedom on the horizon,
our patience is being tried.
Weariness has settled deep in our bones.
Anxiety about the future
robs us of our present joy.
When we live from our souls,
happiness is there.
When we live from our souls,
resilience is there.
When we live from our souls,
patience is there.
When we live from our souls,
hope is there.
We behold the sunrise,
and we behold the sunset;
we gaze at the moon
and see your greater story.
You give us all we need,
and it is enough
to make it through to the finish line.

Together,
we have enough light
to illuminate our next steps.
When we change our story,
we change the world.
Lord, forgive us
when we let the external circumstances
of our life determine
our state of being.
Lord, help us
to see YOUR light
at the end of the tunnel,

Amen.

God of Truth:

It really is simple isn't it?
Whatever we are gazing at,
in any given moment,
ends up being what we pay attention to.
It is all a matter of focus.
We allow our eyes to dart
from one thing to another,
so we don't have to attend
to what truly matters.
We miss so much.
We are ready to embrace a new way of seeing.
We glimpse it in the power of a vaccine
to change our lives
and in the eternal beauty of nature.
We behold it in those
who are devoted to our care
and in the joy-filled faces of children.
Let us not be locked
into our own perception of what we see.
Help us behold a world beyond dominance,
control, fear and insecurity.
Widen our vision,
Lord, to include new possibilities.
When we view the world
through the lens of love
everything is luminous
and infused with significance.

Keep our eyes focused on you!
Only then,
can we see the light
in ourselves
and in one another.

Amen

Living Love:

Lent is calling us to the work of our souls.
We find ourselves clinging
to old anxieties and wading in deep waters.
It requires some heavy lifting
to be the people our world needs now.
Transform us so that we can transform others.
When trust is bent and near breaking
may we be people who reflect your eternal truth.
When politicians fail to lead,
may we stand in the gap,
bringing justice and equity.
When we see great divisions arise
within communities and churches,
may we be bridge builders.
When our hearts are hardened,
may we discover hope in a beloved community.
When the beliefs of our neighbor
fill us with anger,
may we live in a space
of extravagant understanding.
When we see those who are homeless
and without resources,
may our concern give rise to action.
When we are at a loss,
may we open our hands
and release our fear and doubt.

When we are overwhelmed by chaos
may we find solid ground to stand on.
When we want to be heard,
may we choose our words with care.
When we are lonely
may we create places of warmth and laughter.
We acknowledge that grace moves
when we embrace the paradoxes of our lives.

The work
we have been given to do is clear:
We wait.
We endure.
We persist.
We hope.

Amen

Source of Life:

The events of our days
often leave us breathless.
We lose our rhythm.
What if we could just breathe?
Breathe through our anxieties about our children.
Breathe through the sadness of our losses.
Breathe through the impermeable boundaries
of understanding.
Breathe in and breathe out
and listen to the gift we have been given.
Taking delight in being present
right where we are;
all present and accounted for.
Knowing that we have enough
and are enough.
Your eternal mystery
is right here in our breath.
Our ancestors did not speak your name
but breathed it: Yah-weh.
Sacred breath —
you breathe spirit into us
as the oxygen of life.
Breathing in,
we accept life in that moment
and in breathing out we let go.

Yah-weh,
hear our prayers
as they take shape in our souls
and fly to you.
We meet you in that moment.
When we breathe,
we speak your name.
And it is that sound that greets us
when we are born
and heralds the moment
when we leave this world.
Caught the rhythm of our breath,
we fall in love with the present.
We fall in love with the gift of just be-ing
You give us our breath
and we will return it to you

Amen

Holy One:

Circle of love,
widen the capacity of our hearts.
Circle of healing,
mend our brokenness.
Circle of compassion,
increase our patience and our empathy.
Circle of inclusiveness,
destroy the walls we have created.
Circle of solace,
ease our grief and our loss.
Circle of wisdom,
enlighten the hard choices we make.
Circle of hope,
help us, in all things, to choose love.
Circle of protection,
affirm the dignity of all.
Circle of calm,
give us strength for the journey.
Circle of blessing,
renew and sustain our spirits.
Circle of empowerment,
walk with us in the darkness.
Encircle us
so that we might rise
to dance with all
of your Holy creation.

No matter the circumstance.

Amen

Merciful God:

As we embrace this Lenten season,
you invite us to examine
the holy fragments of our lives.
All we knew a year ago
has come undone
and our broken pieces
are laid before us:
Pieces filled with pain.
Pieces worn by weariness.
Pieces shaped by discomfort.
Pieces that have sharp edges.
Pieces broken by grief.
Perhaps, within the pandemic,
you are bringing our pieces together
and shaping new identities.
"Holy disruption" is teaching us that...
Our pieces don't have to line up perfectly.
Our pieces don't have to measure up
to someone else's standard.
Our pieces don't have to follow any formula.
Our pieces are messy,
and they are Holy.
Our pieces are unique,
with their own color,
shape and beauty.
Every piece shines
and every piece belongs.

God,
you are calling all of our
holy fragments
together with love and delight
saying:
You are my beloved!
You are mine!
You who desire wholeness,
create a new
mosaic in our souls.

Amen

Healing and Restoring God:

It has been one year
since we were "called inside."
"Called inside" to protect one another
from a pandemic illness.
"Called inside" to examine the role of our soul.
Called inside to begin
an unbidden personal and spiritual quest.
Your people are always strengthened in exile
where the familiar is taken away.
You were in the first breath we took
when we realized that we were living a new narrative.
You have sustained our breath ever since.
Soon,
as we are slowly called outside again,
we emerge as people reborn.
Who are we now?
We are people who possess a faith
that gets them up in the morning
and peacefully closes their eyes at night.
We are a people called to bring wholeness
to all that is broken.
We are a people who know
that vulnerability and fear
do not have the final say.
We are a people whose Lenten experience
is teaching us to live out the resurrection story.
Your love has sustained us

and given us
unforeseen blessings
in an unforeseen time.
A new horizon awaits us.
How will we walk into it?
We will claim all that we have learned
during this time.
We will warm the spaces
that have been cold
and empty with our love.
We will hold our dear ones close.
We will bring healing
to all those who suffer.
We will renew
the face of the earth.

Amen.

Gracious Creator:

We can feel it.
The fear around our hearts
is beginning to melt.
A glimmer of hope is there
on the horizon,
Emerging slowly,
like the sun returning
after a dark storm.
God, you have sent that light
to shine afresh on the earth.

We peer out from our carefully protected spaces
and wonder how, we too, will emerge.
How, now, will we show up?
Lord, please accompany us as we transition
back to being in the world.

Those first steps will be tentative.
Holding tightly to Your hand, O God,
we will begin to Move.
We will walk in the footsteps of those whom,
during this time,
have shown us the courage
to absorb and transform
our darkness and our despair.
Perhaps, our first steps
will be in a new pattern —

mindfully filled with all we have learned,
and empty of all that no longer serves us.
We will venture out
to touch the Holy Ground of others.

God, we ask you now to listen
to our hesitancy, our vulnerability,
and our doubts.
We ask you to rejoice with us
as our lost experience of Life returns.
Remind us that,
in You,
our struggle is strength on full display.
Help us to remember
that even in our time of lockdown,
Our spirits have always been free.

We fell apart
so we could fall more beautifully together.
Here comes the sun.
It does seem like years since it's been here.
Here comes the sun
and we join our voices
to declare that it is, indeed, all right!

We pray this in all of your Holy Names.
Amen!

Ever Creating God:

Hosana!
We have been waiting
for the glory of Palm Sunday!
We join in the shouting
the acclaim of the
"One who comes in the name of the Lord."
He, who enters Jerusalem
at the beginning of Passover
during the festival of freedom and miracles.
He, who riding on a donkey,
teaches that humility is strength,
and religion cannot be used to justify
unjust economic and social systems.
We are living out this season
of alleluias and rejoicing
that our "still speaking God"
is made manifest.
We have borne witness
to monumental changes and distress.
The veil has been pulled back
to reveal the ways we have
lived in opposition to God's love.
We have persevered through great losses.
We reject a return
to what was considered normal.
We acknowledge the need
to hit the reset button on our world.
Let's stay awake

and embrace the wisdom
that we have gleaned.
Let's clear a space
for a new age of righteousness.
Let's push through our cautiousness
and face each day without pretense.
The Lord has held us in safety.
The Lord has been faithful.
We live in abundance.
We will not restrain our joy.
Our hearts beat with your love.

Amen!

Loving God:

We sing a song of resurrection—
Of joy, Of renewal,
Of long-awaited reunions.
We are being asked
what we have learned.
What do we hold most dear?
What new joy can we share?
What did we abandon along the way?
What do we believe no longer serves
the common good?
We are asked
if resurrection lives in our lives.
Are our hearts now wide enough
to embrace all without exception?
Can we now be restored to one another?
Can we share all that we have?
Can we release our fears?
Can we work for justice?
Can we live in peace?
Can we allow the earth to breathe?
For so long we have waited
for our lives to return.
For so long we have been living
from a place of surrender.
We have begun to see
a new future.
Do we run towards it with abandon
or move cautiously in hope?

Do we have the courage
to live out
the profound lessons
of this time and place?
We rejoice because all things
are becoming new.
We sing our alleluia song.
Arise!

Amen!

God of Courage:

Fear has become
an unwelcome companion,
of late.
It tricks us into thinking
that we are safe.
It clings to us
and we find it hard
to shake ourselves from its grip.
It creates havoc
in our individual
and collective spirits
When we examine our souls deeply,
we see fear in its many disguises.
It lurks in the dark corners.
It separates us from one another
It brings trauma to communities.
It weaponizes words.
It incites violence.
It fuels hatred.
Fear is the container
for all things that are not of God.
Fear does not protect us
from pain or disappointment.
Fear saps our joy.
Fear forces us into life draining choices.
Your love releases
and transforms all fear.

In that love
we can live at the edge
of something great.
Let go
and feel safely held.
You have this.
You have us.
Fear not!

Amen

Sovereign God:

We like to believe the myth
that we are in control,
although evidence is always to the contrary.
We want our belief to be true
because relinquishing control
means we are vulnerable to sickness,
greed, gun violence, hatred,
addiction and environmental devastation.
The horror of evil is, indeed, at work in the world.
But we pay a high price
for our need to be in control.
It is exhausting,
leaving us with little room for prayer,
presence, and compassion.
Holding tight to our sense of security
makes us blind and deaf
to the needs of the world.
We deny the promise of Easter
that death has lost its power.
We need a hard reset —
installing you into our operating systems.
We need to create a greater capacity
for holy possibilities.
When we let go,
something holy is gracefully released
into our spirits.
When we let go,

you join us in co-creation.
When we let go,
we can sense a great awakening.
When we let go,
we come home to ourselves
and to one another.
When we let go,
we are open to the mystery
that holds so much more
than we could ever
bring forth alone.

Take a deep breath.
Let it all go.
We are your own.

Amen

God of the Earth:

We hold out our hands
and touch the blessedness of creation.
We hear your voice in the gentle breeze
whispering the rhythms of renewal and change.
We feel unspeakable joy
as we behold earth's beauty.
Indigenous wisdom speaks to us.
Scientific wisdom speaks to us.
Holy wisdom speaks to us.
We stand upon our most precious gift,
passed from generation to generation.
The earth is sacred
and given to us for safekeeping.
Another Earth Day
has come and gone.
And we continue to squander
the wonder that sustains us.
We spend it like a limitless commodity.
Times such as these
reveal the impact of our neglect and misuse.
Times such as these
reflect the damage we have done.
We ask for help
to roll the stone of our complicity away.
Because we know
that just longing to do things differently
is not enough.

We are being called
to act boldly
calling forth new ways
to love this world to life.
We ask God
to enter the great web of life
with fierce commitment
to sustainable practices.
We ask God
to renew the face of the earth
and those
who are its stewards.

Amen

Co-Creating God:

We are considering what remains
after everything that fell apart
seems to be coming together.
So much has come to light
and we need to be sure
that we are not still in the dark.
Multiple pandemics
have produced a multitude of lessons.
As we begin emerging and reconnecting,
how might we consider
what we are to do with our new-found wisdom?
Our faith tells us
that we cannot let our previous "normal"
cover the face of the earth.
We cannot afford to go back
and let systems hold people hostage.
We have learned that
everything that came apart replicates the whole.
Fires have come under control in some places
only to rage in others.
We are caught between
the joy of what can happen as a result of the vaccine
and the horror of the losses in India
and around the world.
We are caught between the awareness
of racial reckoning
and raw hatred on display.

We are caught between
returning prosperity for some
and great poverty for others.
We want to do more
than to just be survivors of these times.
Jewish teaching invites us
to join you in Tikkun Olam
—the repair the earth.
It is what we are called to do.
Sit in the quiet.
Rest in the questions.
Ponder our lessons.
Disrupt what we have called normal.
Open our hearts
to your prophetic
vision of justice.

Amen

Sustaining God:

Sometimes
we let our world get very small.
It is natural to contain what has been out of control.
Our hearts have been working overtime.
So, we limit what we see.
Sometimes,
we protect ourselves
by keeping what is ugly hidden from view.
We stay safe by staying where we are.
And then, as if by surprise,
it becomes all too clear.
The veil is lifted again.
We see the world,
in its entirety,
and become overwhelmed
by its suffering.
Pandemics
have been at play for centuries
disguised as law, order, and patriotism.
We take for granted
what most people spend their lifetime
wishing for.
As things are opening up for many of us,
they are closing down for others.
While we walk safely in our neighborhoods,
others cannot take one step without fear.

We are protected from the virus
and others continue to die
in great numbers.
Privilege protects many
while others struggle each day to survive.
We want to do better
because what we have experienced
causes us to know better.
We want to be free from placing blame.
We want to be free from conspiring and condemning.
There is so much we don't want to know.
There is so much we don't know how to respond to.
There is so much we are struggling with.
But we do know this:
We are not alone
as we live into this mystery.
WE are the place that you choose to dwell.
You are at work with in us
and around us.
Our hearts can open
to the world again.

Amen

Gracious and Holy God:

We have come so far.
We can't turn back now.
We are survivors
living into our legacy.
We must take our place
in repairing all that has been revealed to us.
Our souls have collided
with the world of sickness, pain and injustice.
We have seen the cost of greed and pride.
The spotlight has been turned on the self for too long.
We must turn to solidarity with "the Other."
The eternal conflict
playing out between Israel and Palestine reminds us.
The great anguish in India reminds us.
Our abundance of vaccine
in the face of suffering reminds us.
We have been saddened,
sobered and summoned to change.
We have experienced grief.
How will we bring comfort to others?
We have lived in fear.
How can we create safe spaces for others?
We have experienced silence.
What words will our new voice speak?
We have experienced loneliness.
What will our new connections look like?
We experienced longing.

What will we do
with our new freedoms?
We have experienced despair.
What hope will we share?
We can no longer say
that we do not see.
You have opened our hearts.
Your grace surrounds us.
We embrace this holy dialogue.
It is our hands
that are needed to heal,
save, and restore.
It is our hands that are needed
to bring peace,
forgiveness, and justice.
We pause with you
at the edge of holiness
and see our new path clearly.
The possibilities are endless.

Amen

Come Holy Spirit Come!

Whisper the words
that we need to hear!
Through the pandemic,
we followed
the pillar of fire through the desert.
Now we are called forth
from the darkness.
At the right time
our hearts experience
Pentecost, anew.
We see a world gathered together
as if in one place.
We feel the same unity
through the sound of all of the world's voices.
We feel the same wind enlarge our souls.
We feel that same spirit touch our hearts.
We feel the torch of that same fire passed to us.
Move within us!
Empower us!
Enliven us!
Open our hands to do your will.
Free us from our noisy minds.
Invite us
to gently follow our own path of engagement
and respect the paths of others.
Expand our circle
of inclusiveness and widen our embrace.

Strengthen our ability
to hold the contradictions of our lives.
Bring us discernment
between the reality
of what should remain
and the dream of what can be.
Our souls are replenished.
The world is filled
with delight and amazement.
We can live
in awe and wonder again.
Come Holy Spirit Come!

Amen

Everlasting God:

Today,
is our national day of remembrance.
We honor those
who have given their lives
to keep our country safe.
At times like these,
we are reminded
that loving our country
means examining its past.
Because the way we hold
our historical memories impacts the future.
We gaze at our national history
with pride
and also confront
that which is shameful in our past.
Often,
we are tempted to turn away
because it is all too painful.
Examining the patterns
of collective greed, fear, and violence
reveal the distance
between our national values
and our actions.
Honest reckoning is redemptive.
Confronting our ghosts
takes courage and honesty.
It is hard and painful work.

And yet,
it is the work
that is ours now to do.
We can reset our national compass
—a compass that can inform wise leadership:
encouraging peace,
providing greater access,
increasing inclusivity,
protecting our planet,
and providing dignity for all.
Our lessons are hidden
in the rearview mirror of our history.
The sacrament of the present
is informed by what memory teaches us.
The greatest way
we can bring honor to the past
is to use it to heal us.

Amen

God of New Life:

We are living in a brave new world.
Some of us are bursting through our doors at breakneck speed.
Some of us are cautiously peeking around corners.
Some of us are doing test drives around the block.
Everything old is new again.
Our words and our actions have renewed power.
Called to new levels of compassion,
it is time to see one another as holy.
Anxiety fuels our narrative.
Concern for others makes us cautious.
Not knowing what is expected
seems to be our new normal.
We lean into the growing edges
of this new space — this brave space.
Like hermit crabs,
who have abandoned their old shells,
we are vulnerable.
What we are becoming is not fully known.
So, we bring who we are to every moment.
We take a deep breath
and offer grace to ourselves.
We offer grace to others.
We suspend judgement
because we never know
the whole story.

Who is fragile?
Who needs our love?
Who is afraid?
Who is grieving?
If we choose to journey together...
ignorance will become understanding,
vulnerability will become confidence,
fear will become faith,
sorrow will become joy,
grieving will become compassion,
This is our rebirthing time,
We will be present,
here and now,
offering all that we have learned.
Living with our hands wide open
and stretched to the sky.
Life, as we know it is calling!

Amen!

God of Peace:

Help us to hear
the wisdom of quiet voices.
We are trying to find our way
through the din of angry rhetoric.
Individual and collective egos
scream for our attention.
Noise is everywhere.
The noise that wants
to return us to the "good old days."
The noise that wants
to move forward at warp speed.
The noise that disregards
the innocent and marginalized.
The noise that would tell us
that the pandemic is over.
The noise that destroys human dignity.
The noise that pollutes the truth.
In the midst of the cacophony of sound,
the essential things become lost
We have questions that search for peace.
The ground we walk on feels shaky.
Our world did not come apart
so that it would stay the same.
This time searches for its legacy.
Help us to find the strength
to drown out the noise.
Reveal yourself to us
in the silence.

It is where we know who we are.
It is where we find clarity.
It is there we find refuge.
It is there we find our way.
Help us to know
the power of quiet conversations.
Quiet spaces
produce voices
of peace and justice.
It is where
our souls find truth.

Amen

Healing God:

Our souls are shifting.
We feel like we live in two worlds.
The one where we live
as if nothing has happened
And...
The one where we are overwhelmed
by the reality of *all* that has happened.
Our brains keep the inner dialogue going.
We are filled with conflict.
Shall we stay in our comfort zone?
Shall we do the deep work
that is before us to do?
We have been through a time
of sacred mystery.
We have been torn and broken
so that we can tend
to the brokenness in others.
We look for the moments
where what we have learned can be used.
Shine a light
on all that we have been taught so painfully.
Help us to know
that we will have the strength
for the fight.
Let us be present to it.
Our souls need tending.

Help us find
those around us
who will help us.
They will feel
like the sunlight enfolding us
and keeping us safe.
Remind us
that our shifting souls
are held by you.
And you will be our guide
through the vulnerable places.

Amen

Ministering Spirit of God:

Our shadows
are always close by.
Buildings collapse.
People perish.
The rich live
at the peril of the poor.
Greed drives profit over lives.
Such things pierce our souls.
It lives within the landscape of our nation.
We have enough people
who know how to make a profit.
We need more people
who take on challenging and holy things.
And we have seen them in the rubble,
doing the work of your love in the world.
They have learned from the present
and know that God walks us into the future.
They know that our God
came to dwell among the powerless.
They help us to carry our wounds with grace.
The muscles of their hearts are expansive and strong.
These are the souls among us who invest in necessary things.
They act upon the yearnings of their spirit and live for others.
Their hands are dirty and their souls are weary.
But they know what love can build.

Amen

Giver of Every Good Gift:

We call ourselves
"The Land of the Free"
and
"The Home of the Brave"
Our national narrative
is at a crossroads
as it has been so many times before.
We are a country
built on brave ideas
and bold concepts.
A land of magnificent possibilities.
A land that we love.
We hold both the dreams and needs
of our country in our hands.
We can no longer afford
to navigate in shallow waters.
We cannot waste time on hollow goals.
We must be about the necessary work of liberty.
This has been a time for listening and taking notes.
Multiple pandemics
have the power to turn us
towards the things that matter.

We are a great evolving experiment
in democracy.
What "truths" do we actually
"hold to be self -evident"?

Can learn from our mistakes,
make reparations,
and rebuild unjust systems?
Can we stand as a nation
whose diversity and inclusivity
are a reflection of strength?
If we move towards hope,
it will take all of our participation
We must trade trust in ourselves
for trust in our collective will.
This land we stand on is not ours
—it was given for our caretaking.
Let us be resolved
to believe
in our resilience once again.
Until the fearful,
abandoned,
and rejected
are filled with access,
hope, and love.

Amen

God of our strength:

Sometimes the pain of the world
seems too much to bear.
The hurt is all around us:
those experiencing loss
of those they love,
those who are ill
because of the politicization
of the pandemic,
those who are the victims of trauma,
those who have lost their ancestral lands
and those who are victims of hate.
Create within us a larger space
to walk with others in their pain.
Only you can offer our souls
a free and enduring upgrade.
Spirit 2.0 is now available to all
who seek your kin-dom.
Install within us a new system that can:
increase the bandwidth
of our hearts for compassion,
create networks
that increase our connectedness,
guard against toxic narratives
and protect our identities
from being consumed by the world.

We crave operating systems that:
replace trendy interests
for deeply lived lives,
replace distraction for reflection,
replace complacency with care,
replace judgement
with compassion
and replace disappointment
with gratitude
Increase our capability
so that we can be the voice
of your good news
and act
with renewed mission
and purpose.
The offer is here!
The offer is now!

Amen

Eternal Light:

We long to BE
the change needed in the world.
Deep change.
Real change.
Change that comes
from being attuned
to the heartaches of the world.
We live in a culture
that has protected injustices
and created anguish.
The long arc of multiple pandemics
is now stretched out before us.
It is you are the path of change.
The world we seek
is one filled with your Beatitudes.
Free us from the parts of ourselves
that are angry at those
whose personal decisions
put our lives at risk.
Free us from the parts of ourselves
that are fearful.
Free us from the parts of ourselves
that are pandemic weary.
Free us from the parts of ourselves
that lack courage.

Take it all, Lord,
and turn it into a collective
call to action.
Because change
is found in your liberation.
Our work is defined by your "kin-dom."
Help us to be the difference
that makes ALL the difference.
Help us to be influencers
that change hearts and minds
for truth.
We cannot wait
because the time is now.
Can we BE the change?
Please, bring it on!

Amen

God of Hope:

We thought the world was changing.
We scan the horizon every day
for any sign of hope.
Is there a glimmer somewhere?
We are learning that
when you value your own independence
over the lives of others, the cost is great.
We are reaping the consequences
of not valuing our interconnectedness.
We are victims of our lack of care for one another.
Sometimes it feels
like we are experiencing
a national dark night of the soul.
Just when we thought we were healing;
old wounds are emerging.
Just when we thought
we were being stitched together;
we are falling apart.
Just when we thought
there was a light at the end of the tunnel;
it is growing dimmer.
Just when we thought
we felt peace;
now panic has emerged again.

What version
of our national self will we choose?

Your beloved community
is our desire.
Give us the strength
to face our collective demons,
repent and begin anew.
Help us to embrace our brokenness,
our messiness and confusion.
For it is here
that the gift of grace is found.
There is good news!
We are greater than our interaction
with the world.
May we hold our words,
and our judgements with humility.
May we remember
that grace is present
in the midst of disappointment.
May we know that
we are on the path
to something new.
We see it there
on the horizon.
Just a glimmer,
but with you,
we know it is there.

Amen

Divine Love:

Every day you fill us
with more evidence
of how deeply woven together we are.
It is our moral imperative
to consider the ways our actions impact others.
True liberty comes clothed in responsibility
for the common good.
When one of us can't breathe,
no one can breathe.
Lies matter and undermine valued institutions.
Our democratic principles
and voting rights are threatened.
The value of one person's free will
trumps the well -being of another.
We allow anger to fuel our discourse.
The cost is so great.
Help us to confront the fabrication of our history
so that we don't repeat the heartaches of the past.
Help us to understand that there is no room
for exceptionalism in your world.
Help us to not confuse the American way of life
with Your kin-dom.
Comfort and easy answers
put the world at peril.
We must live in the midst of heartache
until we learn the lessons that will move us forward in love.
We must participate in the pain of the world if it is to change.

This love you so bountifully share with us
is to be shared with others.
It is that connection that stretches our soul.
It is that connection
that harnesses the power of human potential.
It is that connection
that heals the human spirit and makes us whole.
Help us act in ways
that acknowledge that all people
are made in your image.
Help us to live out the universality of your love.
Help us to see a world
where we all cross the finish line together.
Such connections are your holy ground.

Amen

Loving Creator:

In the end,
you will not ask us
how well we entertained our freedoms.
Instead, you will ask us
how well we loved
our brothers and sisters.
The choices that we make,
for reasons known only to ourselves,
are accountable to all.
Because we do not cherish
our connectedness,
our pandemic history
is repeating itself.
How did we get here, Lord?
What was inevitable
was made preventable.
And now we ache
from the knowledge
that life is repeating itself.
Last time we were unified in our dismay.
This time we are divided.
We leave teachers,
healthcare professionals
and front-line workers
to carry the burden
of our choices.

Climate change robs people
of their homes and livelihoods.
Again, you lay before us
the great lesson of this time
with the hope
that we will listen.
The enormity
of what faces us
means that we dare not live
independent lives.
Open our hearts to you
so that we can open them
to one another.
Open our hearts
to the dignity in all life.
Open our hearts
to participate in countless,
quiet acts of love.
Open our hearts
to see beyond
our own interests
to the interests of all.
Our hope
rests in lives
lived for one another.

Amen

God of Gratitude:

We came together
to pray
when the world began to change.
We came with hearts broken
and vulnerable.
We came to cry out for justice.
We came whipped
by the winds of chaos
to ground ourselves in love.
We came to raise our Ebenezer,
a stone of hope,
amid arid soil.
We went where we could share
our hurts together
and found the world bearable.
As we turned one another's faces to you.
We uncovered our brave space.
We discovered that joy and love
could be its own revolution.
We claimed healing and rest.
We learned to live
our resiliency out loud.
We celebrated acts
of goodness.
We bore witness
to the possible.

We recovered beauty
in the world
We found lights of hope
and wonder.
God gave us to one another
in times such as these.
We found that
because you held us,
we could hold one another.
So that together,
we could find ourselves
tied together
with heartstrings.

Amen

EPILOGUE

If these prayers have fed your soul and helped you find peace and significance during these tumultuous times, please consider sharing The Light Between Us: Praying in Times Such As These with friends and colleagues. And if you are so moved, posting a review somewhere, especially on Facebook and Amazon can go a long way toward getting these prayers out into greater visibility and circulation.

For those who have been inspired to begin their own prayer vigil community, the author is available to provide ideas and advice in launching similar new groups.

For those who would like to use the book as the topic of a study for a discussion group, the author would be pleased to provide discussion questions for your use:

You can contact Amy Duncan by email:

4thelightbetweenus@gmail.com

Made in the USA
Las Vegas, NV
14 April 2022